Date: _____

Quote Of The Day

_____
_____

Today I am truly grateful for...
_____
_____
_____
_____

Here's what would make today great...
_____
_____
_____
_____

I am...
_____
_____
_____

Some amazing things that happened today...
_____
_____

Some amazing things that happened today...
_____
_____

What could I have done to make today even better?
_____
_____

Date: ☼

Quote Of The Day

_____

_____

Today I am truly grateful for...

_____

_____

_____

_____

_____

Here's what would make today great...

_____

_____

_____

_____

_____

I am...

_____

_____

_____

Some amazing things that happened today...

_____

_____

Some amazing things that happened today...   ✦ ✦ 🌙

_____

_____

What could I have done to make today even better?

_____

_____

Date: ....

Quote Of The Day

_____
_____

Today I am truly grateful for...

_____
_____
_____
_____

Here's what would make today great...

_____
_____
_____
_____
_____

I am...

_____
_____
_____

Some amazing things that happened today...

_____
_____

Some amazing things that happened today...

_____
_____

What could I have done to make today even better?

_____
_____

Date:

Quote Of The Day

_____
_____
_____

Today I am truly grateful for...

_____
_____
_____
_____

Here's what would make today great...

_____
_____
_____
_____

I am...

_____
_____

Some amazing things that happened today...

_____
_____

Some amazing things that happened today...

_____
_____

What could I have done to make today even better?

_____

Date: _____ ☀

Quote Of The Day

_____
_____
_____

Today I am truly grateful for...

_____
_____
_____
_____
_____
_____

Here's what would make today great...

_____
_____
_____
_____
_____
_____

I am...

_____
_____
_____
_____

Some amazing things that happened today...

_____
_____

Some amazing things that happened today...   ✦ ✦ 🌙

_____
_____

What could I have done to make today even better?

_____
_____

Date:

Quote Of The Day

_____

_____

_____

Today I am truly grateful for...

_____

_____

_____

_____

_____

Here's what would make today great...

_____

_____

_____

_____

_____

I am...

_____

_____

_____

Some amazing things that happened today...

_____

_____

Some amazing things that happened today...

_____

_____

What could I have done to make today even better?

_____

_____

Date: _____

Quote Of The Day

_____

_____

_____

Today I am truly grateful for...

_____

_____

_____

_____

_____

Here's what would make today great...

_____

_____

_____

_____

_____

I am...

_____

_____

_____

Some amazing things that happened today...

_____

_____

Some amazing things that happened today...

_____

_____

_____

What could I have done to make today even better?

_____

_____

Date: _____

Quote Of The Day

_____

_____

Today I am truly grateful for...

_____

_____

_____

_____

_____

Here's what would make today great...

_____

_____

_____

_____

_____

I am...

_____

_____

_____

Some amazing things that happened today...

_____

_____

Some amazing things that happened today...

_____

_____

What could I have done to make today even better?

_____

_____

Date: ☼

Quote Of The Day

_____
_____
_____

Today I am truly grateful for...

_____
_____
_____
_____

Here's what would make today great...

_____
_____
_____
_____

I am...

_____
_____

Some amazing things that happened today...

_____
_____

Some amazing things that happened today...

_____
_____

What could I have done to make today even better?

_____
_____

Date:

Quote Of The Day

_____
_____

_____

Today I am truly grateful for...

_____
_____
_____
_____
_____

Here's what would make today great...

_____
_____
_____
_____
_____

I am...

_____
_____
_____

Some amazing things that happened today...

_____
_____

Some amazing things that happened today...

_____
_____
_____

What could I have done to make today even better?

_____
_____

Date: _____ ☀

Quote Of The Day

_____

_____

_____

Today I am truly grateful for...

_____

_____

_____

_____

_____

Here's what would make today great...

_____

_____

_____

_____

_____

I am...

_____

_____

_____

Some amazing things that happened today...

_____

_____

Some amazing things that happened today...   ✦ ✦ 🌙

_____

_____

What could I have done to make today even better?

_____

_____

Date: ☀️

Quote Of The Day

_____
_____
_____

Today I am truly grateful for...

_____
_____
_____
_____
_____

Here's what would make today great...

_____
_____
_____
_____
_____

I am...

_____
_____
_____

Some amazing things that happened today...

_____
_____

Some amazing things that happened today...   ✨ ✨ 🌙

_____
_____

What could I have done to make today even better?

_____
_____

Date: _____

☀

Quote Of The Day

_____
_____
_____

Today I am truly grateful for...

_____
_____
_____
_____
_____

Here's what would make today great...

_____
_____
_____
_____
_____

I am...

_____
_____
_____

Some amazing things that happened today...

_____
_____

Some amazing things that happened today...   ✦ ✦ ☽

_____
_____

What could I have done to make today even better?

_____

Date:

Quote Of The Day

_____
_____

Today I am truly grateful for...

_____
_____
_____
_____

Here's what would make today great...

_____
_____
_____
_____

I am...

_____
_____

Some amazing things that happened today...

_____
_____

Some amazing things that happened today...

_____
_____

What could I have done to make today even better?

_____
_____

Date: _____

☀

Quote Of The Day

_____

_____

Today I am truly grateful for...

_____

_____

_____

_____

Here's what would make today great...

_____

_____

_____

_____

I am...

_____

_____

Some amazing things that happened today...

_____

_____

Some amazing things that happened today...

_____

_____

What could I have done to make today even better?

_____

Date:

Quote Of The Day

_____

_____

_____

Today I am truly grateful for...

_____

_____

_____

_____

_____

Here's what would make today great...

_____

_____

_____

_____

_____

I am...

_____

_____

_____

Some amazing things that happened today...

_____

_____

Some amazing things that happened today...

_____

_____

What could I have done to make today even better?

_____

_____

Date: _____

Quote Of The Day

_____

_____

_____

Today I am truly grateful for...

_____

_____

_____

_____

_____

Here's what would make today great...

_____

_____

_____

_____

_____

I am...

_____

_____

_____

Some amazing things that happened today...

_____

_____

Some amazing things that happened today...

_____

_____

_____

What could I have done to make today even better?

_____

_____

Date:

Quote Of The Day

_____
_____
_____

Today I am truly grateful for...

_____
_____
_____
_____
_____

Here's what would make today great...

_____
_____
_____
_____
_____

I am...

_____
_____
_____

Some amazing things that happened today...

_____
_____

Some amazing things that happened today...

_____
_____

What could I have done to make today even better?

_____
_____

Date:

_____
_____
_____

Today I am truly grateful for...

_____
_____
_____
_____
_____

Here's what would make today great...

_____
_____
_____
_____
_____

I am...

_____
_____
_____

Some amazing things that happened today...

_____
_____

Some amazing things that happened today...

_____
_____
_____

What could I have done to make today even better?

_____
_____

Date: ☀

Quote Of The Day

_____
_____
_____

Today I am truly grateful for...

_____
_____
_____
_____
_____

Here's what would make today great...

_____
_____
_____
_____
_____

I am...

_____
_____
_____

Some amazing things that happened today...

_____
_____

Some amazing things that happened today...   ✨ ✨ 🌙

_____
_____

What could I have done to make today even better?

_____
_____

Date: ⋯⋯⋯⋯⋯⋯⋯⋯⋯⋯⋯⋯

Quote Of The Day

Today I am truly grateful for...

Here's what would make today great...

I am...

Some amazing things that happened today...

Some amazing things that happened today...

What could I have done to make today even better?

Date:

Quote Of The Day

_____

_____

Today I am truly grateful for...

_____

_____

_____

_____

Here's what would make today great...

_____

_____

_____

_____

I am...

_____

_____

Some amazing things that happened today...

_____

_____

Some amazing things that happened today...

_____

_____

What could I have done to make today even better?

_____

_____

Date: ☼

Quote Of The Day

_____

_____

_____

Today I am truly grateful for...

_____

_____

_____

_____

_____

Here's what would make today great...

_____

_____

_____

_____

_____

I am...

_____

_____

_____

Some amazing things that happened today...

_____

_____

Some amazing things that happened today... ✦ ✦ ☾

_____

_____

_____

What could I have done to make today even better?

_____

_____

Date:

Quote Of The Day

_____
_____
_____

Today I am truly grateful for...

_____
_____
_____
_____
_____

Here's what would make today great...

_____
_____
_____
_____
_____

I am...

_____
_____
_____

Some amazing things that happened today...

_____
_____

Some amazing things that happened today...

_____
_____

What could I have done to make today even better?

_____
_____

Date: _____

Quote Of The Day

_____
_____
_____

Today I am truly grateful for...

_____
_____
_____
_____
_____
_____

Here's what would make today great...

_____
_____
_____
_____
_____
_____

I am...

_____
_____
_____

Some amazing things that happened today...

_____
_____

Some amazing things that happened today...   ✦ ✦ 🌙

_____
_____

What could I have done to make today even better?

_____
_____

Date: ⌣☀

Quote Of The Day

_____
_____

Today I am truly grateful for...

_____
_____
_____
_____

Here's what would make today great...

_____
_____
_____
_____

I am...

_____
_____

Some amazing things that happened today...

_____

Some amazing things that happened today...   ✦ ✦ ☽

_____
_____

What could I have done to make today even better?

_____

Date: _____

Quote Of The Day

_____

_____

_____

Today I am truly grateful for...

_____

_____

_____

_____

_____

Here's what would make today great...

_____

_____

_____

_____

_____

I am...

_____

_____

Some amazing things that happened today...

_____

_____

Some amazing things that happened today...

_____

_____

What could I have done to make today even better?

_____

Date: ☀️

Quote Of The Day

_____
_____
_____

Today I am truly grateful for...

_____
_____
_____
_____
_____

Here's what would make today great...

_____
_____
_____
_____
_____

I am...

_____
_____
_____

Some amazing things that happened today...

_____
_____

Some amazing things that happened today...   🌙

_____
_____

What could I have done to make today even better?

_____
_____

Date: _____   ☀

Quote Of The Day

_____

_____

_____

Today I am truly grateful for...

_____

_____

_____

_____

_____

Here's what would make today great...

_____

_____

_____

_____

_____

I am...

_____

_____

_____

Some amazing things that happened today...

_____

_____

Some amazing things that happened today...   ✦ ✦ 🌙

_____

_____

What could I have done to make today even better?

_____

_____

Date:

Quote Of The Day

_____
_____
_____

Today I am truly grateful for...

_____
_____
_____
_____
_____

Here's what would make today great...

_____
_____
_____
_____
_____

I am...

_____
_____
_____

Some amazing things that happened today...

_____
_____

Some amazing things that happened today...

_____
_____
_____

What could I have done to make today even better?

_____
_____

Date:

Quote Of The Day

_____
_____
_____

Today I am truly grateful for...

_____
_____
_____
_____
_____

Here's what would make today great...

_____
_____
_____
_____
_____

I am...

_____
_____
_____

Some amazing things that happened today...

_____
_____

Some amazing things that happened today...

_____
_____

What could I have done to make today even better?

_____
_____

Date:

Quote Of The Day

_____
_____

Today I am truly grateful for...

_____
_____
_____
_____

Here's what would make today great...

_____
_____
_____
_____

I am...

_____
_____

Some amazing things that happened today...

_____
_____

Some amazing things that happened today...

_____
_____

What could I have done to make today even better?

_____

Date: ☀

Quote Of The Day

_____
_____
_____

Today I am truly grateful for...

_____
_____
_____
_____
_____

Here's what would make today great...

_____
_____
_____
_____
_____

I am...

_____
_____
_____

Some amazing things that happened today...

_____
_____

Some amazing things that happened today...   ✦ ✦ 🌙

_____
_____

What could I have done to make today even better?

_____
_____

Date:

Quote Of The Day

_____
_____
_____

Today I am truly grateful for...

_____
_____
_____
_____
_____
_____

Here's what would make today great...

_____
_____
_____
_____
_____
_____

I am...

_____
_____
_____

Some amazing things that happened today...

_____
_____
_____

Some amazing things that happened today...

_____
_____
_____

What could I have done to make today even better?

_____
_____

Date: _____

Quote Of The Day

_____
_____
_____

Today I am truly grateful for...

_____
_____
_____
_____
_____
_____

Here's what would make today great...

_____
_____
_____
_____
_____

I am...

_____
_____
_____

Some amazing things that happened today...

_____
_____

Some amazing things that happened today...

_____
_____
_____

What could I have done to make today even better?

_____
_____

Date:

Quote Of The Day

_____

_____

_____

Today I am truly grateful for...

_____

_____

_____

_____

_____

Here's what would make today great...

_____

_____

_____

_____

_____

I am...

_____

_____

_____

Some amazing things that happened today...

_____

_____

Some amazing things that happened today...

_____

_____

What could I have done to make today even better?

_____

Date: _____

Quote Of The Day

_____

_____

_____

Today I am truly grateful for...

_____

_____

_____

_____

_____

Here's what would make today great...

_____

_____

_____

_____

_____

I am...

_____

_____

_____

Some amazing things that happened today...

_____

_____

Some amazing things that happened today...

_____

_____

What could I have done to make today even better?

_____

_____

Date: _____

☀

Quote Of The Day

_____
_____

Today I am truly grateful for...

_____
_____
_____
_____

Here's what would make today great...

_____
_____
_____
_____
_____

I am...

_____
_____
_____

Some amazing things that happened today...

_____
_____

Some amazing things that happened today...

_____
_____
_____

What could I have done to make today even better?

_____
_____

Date: ☀

Quote Of The Day

Today I am truly grateful for...

Here's what would make today great...

I am...

Some amazing things that happened today...

Some amazing things that happened today... ✨ ✨ 🌙

What could I have done to make today even better?

Date:

Quote Of The Day

_____
_____
_____

Today I am truly grateful for...

_____
_____
_____
_____
_____

Here's what would make today great...

_____
_____
_____
_____
_____

I am...

_____
_____
_____

Some amazing things that happened today...

_____
_____

Some amazing things that happened today...

_____
_____
_____

What could I have done to make today even better?

_____
_____

Date:

Quote Of The Day

_____

_____

Today I am truly grateful for...

_____

_____

_____

_____

_____

Here's what would make today great...

_____

_____

_____

_____

_____

I am...

_____

_____

_____

Some amazing things that happened today...

_____

_____

Some amazing things that happened today...

_____

_____

What could I have done to make today even better?

_____

_____

Date:

Quote Of The Day

_____

_____

Today I am truly grateful for...

_____

_____

_____

_____

Here's what would make today great...

_____

_____

_____

_____

I am...

_____

_____

Some amazing things that happened today...

_____

_____

Some amazing things that happened today...

_____

_____

What could I have done to make today even better?

_____

_____

Date:

Quote Of The Day

_____

_____

Today I am truly grateful for...

_____

_____

_____

_____

Here's what would make today great...

_____

_____

_____

_____

I am...

_____

_____

Some amazing things that happened today...

_____

_____

Some amazing things that happened today...

_____

_____

What could I have done to make today even better?

_____

_____

Date:

Quote Of The Day

_____

_____

_____

Today I am truly grateful for...

_____

_____

_____

_____

_____

Here's what would make today great...

_____

_____

_____

_____

_____

I am...

_____

_____

_____

Some amazing things that happened today...

_____

_____

Some amazing things that happened today...

_____

_____

What could I have done to make today even better?

_____

_____

Date: ☀

Quote Of The Day

_____

_____

Today I am truly grateful for...

_____

_____

_____

_____

Here's what would make today great...

_____

_____

_____

_____

I am...

_____

_____

Some amazing things that happened today...

_____

_____

Some amazing things that happened today...   ✦ ✦ 🌙

_____

_____

What could I have done to make today even better?

_____

Date:

Quote Of The Day

_____
_____
_____

Today I am truly grateful for...

_____
_____
_____
_____
_____

Here's what would make today great...

_____
_____
_____
_____
_____

I am...

_____
_____
_____

Some amazing things that happened today...

_____
_____

Some amazing things that happened today...

_____
_____
_____

What could I have done to make today even better?

_____
_____

Date: _____

Quote Of The Day

_____

_____

_____

Today I am truly grateful for...

_____

_____

_____

_____

_____

Here's what would make today great...

_____

_____

_____

_____

_____

I am...

_____

_____

_____

Some amazing things that happened today...

_____

_____

Some amazing things that happened today...

_____

_____

_____

What could I have done to make today even better?

_____

_____

Date:

Quote Of The Day

_____
_____
_____

Today I am truly grateful for...

_____
_____
_____
_____
_____

Here's what would make today great...

_____
_____
_____
_____
_____

I am...

_____
_____
_____

Some amazing things that happened today...

_____
_____

Some amazing things that happened today...

_____
_____

What could I have done to make today even better?

_____
_____

Date: _____

Quote Of The Day

_____

_____

_____

Today I am truly grateful for...

_____

_____

_____

_____

_____

_____

Here's what would make today great...

_____

_____

_____

_____

_____

_____

I am...

_____

_____

_____

Some amazing things that happened today...

_____

_____

Some amazing things that happened today...

_____

_____

_____

What could I have done to make today even better?

_____

_____

Date: ☀

Quote Of The Day

_____
_____

Today I am truly grateful for...

_____
_____
_____
_____
_____

Here's what would make today great...

_____
_____
_____
_____
_____

I am...

_____
_____
_____

Some amazing things that happened today...

_____
_____

Some amazing things that happened today...   ✦ ✦ 🌙

_____
_____

What could I have done to make today even better?

_____

Date:

Quote Of The Day

Today I am truly grateful for...

Here's what would make today great...

I am...

Some amazing things that happened today...

Some amazing things that happened today...

What could I have done to make today even better?

Date: _____

Quote Of The Day

_____
_____
_____

Today I am truly grateful for...

_____
_____
_____
_____
_____

Here's what would make today great...

_____
_____
_____
_____
_____

I am...

_____
_____
_____

Some amazing things that happened today...

_____
_____

Some amazing things that happened today...

_____
_____
_____

What could I have done to make today even better?

_____
_____

Date:

Quote Of The Day

_____

_____

_____

Today I am truly grateful for...

_____

_____

_____

_____

_____

Here's what would make today great...

_____

_____

_____

_____

_____

I am...

_____

_____

_____

Some amazing things that happened today...

_____

_____

Some amazing things that happened today...

_____

_____

_____

What could I have done to make today even better?

_____

_____

Date:

Quote Of The Day

_____
_____
_____

Today I am truly grateful for...

_____
_____
_____
_____
_____

Here's what would make today great...

_____
_____
_____
_____
_____

I am...

_____
_____
_____

Some amazing things that happened today...

_____
_____

Some amazing things that happened today...

_____
_____

What could I have done to make today even better?

_____
_____

Date: _____

Quote Of The Day

_____
_____
_____

Today I am truly grateful for...

_____
_____
_____
_____
_____

Here's what would make today great...

_____
_____
_____
_____
_____

I am...

_____
_____
_____

Some amazing things that happened today...

_____
_____

Some amazing things that happened today...

_____
_____

What could I have done to make today even better?

_____
_____

Date: _____

Quote Of The Day

_____
_____

Today I am truly grateful for...

_____
_____
_____
_____

Here's what would make today great...

_____
_____
_____
_____

I am...

_____
_____

Some amazing things that happened today...

_____
_____

Some amazing things that happened today...

_____
_____

What could I have done to make today even better?

_____

Date:

Quote Of The Day

_____
_____

_____

Today I am truly grateful for...

_____
_____
_____
_____

Here's what would make today great...

_____
_____
_____
_____
_____

I am...

_____
_____

Some amazing things that happened today...

_____
_____

Some amazing things that happened today...

_____
_____

What could I have done to make today even better?

_____
_____

Date: _____

Quote Of The Day

_____

_____

_____

Today I am truly grateful for...

_____

_____

_____

_____

_____

Here's what would make today great...

_____

_____

_____

_____

_____

I am...

_____

_____

_____

Some amazing things that happened today...

_____

_____

Some amazing things that happened today...

_____

_____

What could I have done to make today even better?

_____

Date: _____

☀

Quote Of The Day

_____
_____
_____

Today I am truly grateful for...

_____
_____
_____
_____
_____
_____

Here's what would make today great...

_____
_____
_____
_____
_____
_____

I am...

_____
_____
_____

Some amazing things that happened today...

_____
_____

Some amazing things that happened today...

_____
_____

What could I have done to make today even better?

_____
_____

Date: ☀

Quote Of The Day

_____

_____

Today I am truly grateful for...

_____

_____

_____

_____

Here's what would make today great...

_____

_____

_____

_____

I am...

_____

_____

Some amazing things that happened today...

_____

_____

Some amazing things that happened today... ✨ ✨ 🌙

_____

_____

What could I have done to make today even better?

_____

_____

Date:

Quote Of The Day

_____

_____

Today I am truly grateful for...

_____

_____

_____

_____

Here's what would make today great...

_____

_____

_____

_____

I am...

_____

_____

Some amazing things that happened today...

_____

_____

Some amazing things that happened today...

_____

_____

What could I have done to make today even better?

_____

_____

Date:

Quote Of The Day

_____

_____

Today I am truly grateful for...

_____

_____

_____

_____

Here's what would make today great...

_____

_____

_____

_____

I am...

_____

_____

_____

Some amazing things that happened today...

_____

_____

Some amazing things that happened today...

_____

_____

What could I have done to make today even better?

_____

_____

Date: ☀

Quote Of The Day

_____

_____

Today I am truly grateful for...

_____

_____

_____

_____

Here's what would make today great...

_____

_____

_____

_____

I am...

_____

_____

Some amazing things that happened today...

_____

_____

Some amazing things that happened today...   ✦ ✦ 🌙

_____

_____

What could I have done to make today even better?

_____

Date: _____

Quote Of The Day

_____
_____
_____

Today I am truly grateful for...

_____
_____
_____
_____
_____

Here's what would make today great...

_____
_____
_____
_____
_____

I am...

_____
_____
_____

Some amazing things that happened today...

_____
_____

Some amazing things that happened today...

_____
_____

What could I have done to make today even better?

_____
_____

Date: _____

Quote Of The Day

_____

_____

_____

Today I am truly grateful for...

_____

_____

_____

_____

_____

_____

Here's what would make today great...

_____

_____

_____

_____

_____

I am...

_____

_____

_____

Some amazing things that happened today...

_____

_____

Some amazing things that happened today...

_____

_____

What could I have done to make today even better?

_____

_____

Date:

Quote Of The Day

_____
_____
_____

Today I am truly grateful for...

_____
_____
_____
_____
_____

Here's what would make today great...

_____
_____
_____
_____
_____

I am...

_____
_____
_____

Some amazing things that happened today...

_____
_____

Some amazing things that happened today...

_____
_____
_____

What could I have done to make today even better?

_____
_____

Date:

Quote Of The Day

_____

_____

Today I am truly grateful for...

_____

_____

_____

_____

Here's what would make today great...

_____

_____

_____

_____

_____

I am...

_____

_____

Some amazing things that happened today...

_____

_____

Some amazing things that happened today...

_____

_____

What could I have done to make today even better?

_____

_____

Date:

Quote Of The Day

_____

_____

Today I am truly grateful for...

_____

_____

_____

_____

Here's what would make today great...

_____

_____

_____

_____

I am...

_____

_____

Some amazing things that happened today...

_____

_____

Some amazing things that happened today...

_____

_____

What could I have done to make today even better?

_____

_____

Date:

Quote Of The Day

_____

_____

_____

Today I am truly grateful for...

_____

_____

_____

_____

_____

Here's what would make today great...

_____

_____

_____

_____

_____

I am...

_____

_____

Some amazing things that happened today...

_____

_____

Some amazing things that happened today...

_____

_____

What could I have done to make today even better?

_____

_____

Date: _____ ☀

Quote Of The Day

_____
_____
_____

Today I am truly grateful for...

_____
_____
_____
_____
_____

Here's what would make today great...

_____
_____
_____
_____
_____

I am...

_____
_____
_____

Some amazing things that happened today...

_____
_____

Some amazing things that happened today...   ✨ ✨ 🌙

_____
_____

What could I have done to make today even better?

_____
_____

Date: _____

Quote Of The Day

_____

_____

Today I am truly grateful for...

_____

_____

_____

_____

Here's what would make today great...

_____

_____

_____

_____

I am...

_____

_____

Some amazing things that happened today...

_____

_____

Some amazing things that happened today...

_____

_____

What could I have done to make today even better?

_____

_____

Date:

Quote Of The Day

_____
_____
_____

Today I am truly grateful for...

_____
_____
_____
_____
_____

Here's what would make today great...

_____
_____
_____
_____
_____

I am...

_____
_____
_____

Some amazing things that happened today...

_____
_____

Some amazing things that happened today...

_____
_____

What could I have done to make today even better?

_____
_____

Date:

Quote Of The Day

_____

_____

Today I am truly grateful for...

_____

_____

_____

_____

_____

Here's what would make today great...

_____

_____

_____

_____

_____

I am...

_____

_____

_____

Some amazing things that happened today...

_____

_____

Some amazing things that happened today...

_____

_____

What could I have done to make today even better?

_____

_____

Date: _____

Quote Of The Day

_____
_____
_____

Today I am truly grateful for...

_____
_____
_____
_____
_____

Here's what would make today great...

_____
_____
_____
_____
_____

I am...

_____
_____
_____

Some amazing things that happened today...

_____
_____

Some amazing things that happened today...

_____
_____

What could I have done to make today even better?

_____
_____

Date: _____

Quote Of The Day

_____

_____

_____

Today I am truly grateful for...

_____

_____

_____

_____

_____

Here's what would make today great...

_____

_____

_____

_____

_____

I am...

_____

_____

Some amazing things that happened today...

_____

_____

Some amazing things that happened today...

_____

_____

What could I have done to make today even better?

_____

_____

Date:

Quote Of The Day

_____

_____

Today I am truly grateful for...

_____

_____

_____

_____

Here's what would make today great...

_____

_____

_____

_____

I am...

_____

_____

Some amazing things that happened today...

_____

_____

Some amazing things that happened today...

_____

_____

What could I have done to make today even better?

_____

_____

Date: _____

Quote Of The Day

_____
_____
_____

Today I am truly grateful for...

_____
_____
_____
_____
_____
_____

Here's what would make today great...

_____
_____
_____
_____
_____
_____

I am...

_____
_____
_____

Some amazing things that happened today...

_____
_____

Some amazing things that happened today...

_____
_____
_____

What could I have done to make today even better?

_____
_____

Date: _____ ☀

Quote Of The Day
_____
_____

Today I am truly grateful for...
_____
_____
_____
_____

Here's what would make today great...
_____
_____
_____
_____

I am...
_____
_____

Some amazing things that happened today...
_____
_____

Some amazing things that happened today...
_____
_____

What could I have done to make today even better?
_____
_____

Date: _____ ☀

Quote Of The Day

_____

_____

_____

Today I am truly grateful for...

_____

_____

_____

_____

_____

Here's what would make today great...

_____

_____

_____

_____

_____

I am...

_____

_____

_____

Some amazing things that happened today...

_____

_____

Some amazing things that happened today...   ✨ ✨ 🌙

_____

_____

What could I have done to make today even better?

_____

Date:

Quote Of The Day

_____
_____

Today I am truly grateful for...

_____
_____
_____
_____

Here's what would make today great...

_____
_____
_____
_____

I am...

_____
_____

Some amazing things that happened today...

_____

Some amazing things that happened today...

_____
_____

What could I have done to make today even better?

_____
_____

Date: _____

Quote Of The Day

_____
_____
_____

Today I am truly grateful for...

_____
_____
_____
_____
_____

Here's what would make today great...

_____
_____
_____
_____
_____

I am...

_____
_____
_____

Some amazing things that happened today...

_____
_____

Some amazing things that happened today...

_____
_____

What could I have done to make today even better?

_____
_____

Date:

Quote Of The Day

_____
_____
_____

Today I am truly grateful for...

_____
_____
_____
_____

Here's what would make today great...

_____
_____
_____
_____
_____

I am...

_____
_____
_____

Some amazing things that happened today...

_____
_____

Some amazing things that happened today...

_____
_____

What could I have done to make today even better?

_____
_____

Date: _____

☀

Quote Of The Day

_____
_____
_____

Today I am truly grateful for...

_____
_____
_____
_____
_____

Here's what would make today great...

_____
_____
_____
_____
_____

I am...

_____
_____
_____

Some amazing things that happened today...

_____
_____

Some amazing things that happened today...

_____
_____

What could I have done to make today even better?

_____
_____

Date: _____

Quote Of The Day
_____
_____
_____

Today I am truly grateful for...
_____
_____
_____
_____
_____

Here's what would make today great...
_____
_____
_____
_____
_____

I am...
_____
_____
_____

Some amazing things that happened today...
_____
_____

Some amazing things that happened today...
_____
_____
_____

What could I have done to make today even better?
_____
_____

Date:

Quote Of The Day

_____

_____

Today I am truly grateful for...

_____

_____

_____

_____

Here's what would make today great...

_____

_____

_____

_____

I am...

_____

_____

Some amazing things that happened today...

_____

_____

Some amazing things that happened today...

_____

_____

What could I have done to make today even better?

_____

_____

Date:

Quote Of The Day

_____
_____

Today I am truly grateful for...

_____
_____
_____
_____
_____

Here's what would make today great...

_____
_____
_____
_____
_____

I am...

_____
_____
_____

Some amazing things that happened today...

_____
_____

Some amazing things that happened today...

_____
_____

What could I have done to make today even better?

_____
_____

Date:

Quote Of The Day

_____

_____

Today I am truly grateful for...

_____

_____

_____

_____

Here's what would make today great...

_____

_____

_____

_____

_____

I am...

_____

_____

_____

Some amazing things that happened today...

_____

_____

Some amazing things that happened today...

_____

_____

_____

What could I have done to make today even better?

_____

_____

Date: _____

☀

Quote Of The Day

_____
_____
_____

Today I am truly grateful for...

_____
_____
_____
_____
_____

Here's what would make today great...

_____
_____
_____
_____
_____

I am...

_____
_____
_____

Some amazing things that happened today...

_____
_____

Some amazing things that happened today...

_____
_____
_____

What could I have done to make today even better?

_____
_____

Date: ☀

Quote Of The Day

_____

_____

Today I am truly grateful for...

_____

_____

_____

_____

Here's what would make today great...

_____

_____

_____

_____

I am...

_____

_____

Some amazing things that happened today...

_____

_____

Some amazing things that happened today...   ✦ ✦ 🌙

_____

_____

What could I have done to make today even better?

_____

_____

Date: _____

Quote Of The Day

_____

_____

_____

Today I am truly grateful for...

_____

_____

_____

_____

_____

Here's what would make today great...

_____

_____

_____

_____

_____

I am...

_____

_____

_____

Some amazing things that happened today...

_____

_____

Some amazing things that happened today...

_____

_____

_____

What could I have done to make today even better?

_____

_____

Date: _____

Quote Of The Day

_____
_____
_____

Today I am truly grateful for...

_____
_____
_____
_____
_____
_____

Here's what would make today great...

_____
_____
_____
_____
_____
_____

I am...

_____
_____
_____
_____

Some amazing things that happened today...

_____
_____
_____

Some amazing things that happened today...

_____
_____
_____

What could I have done to make today even better?

_____
_____

Date: _____

Quote Of The Day

_____

_____

_____

Today I am truly grateful for...

_____

_____

_____

_____

_____

Here's what would make today great...

_____

_____

_____

_____

_____

I am...

_____

_____

_____

Some amazing things that happened today...

_____

_____

Some amazing things that happened today...

_____

_____

What could I have done to make today even better?

_____

_____

Date: ....

Quote Of The Day

_____

_____

_____

Today I am truly grateful for...

_____

_____

_____

_____

_____

Here's what would make today great...

_____

_____

_____

_____

_____

I am...

_____

_____

Some amazing things that happened today...

_____

_____

Some amazing things that happened today...

_____

_____

What could I have done to make today even better?

_____

_____

Date: _____

Quote Of The Day

_____

_____

_____

Today I am truly grateful for...

_____

_____

_____

_____

_____

Here's what would make today great...

_____

_____

_____

_____

_____

I am...

_____

_____

_____

Some amazing things that happened today...

_____

_____

Some amazing things that happened today...

_____

_____

_____

What could I have done to make today even better?

_____

_____

Date: _____

Quote Of The Day

_____
_____
_____

Today I am truly grateful for...

_____
_____
_____
_____
_____

Here's what would make today great...

_____
_____
_____
_____
_____

I am...

_____
_____
_____

Some amazing things that happened today...

_____
_____

Some amazing things that happened today...

_____
_____
_____

What could I have done to make today even better?

_____
_____

Date: ☀

Quote Of The Day

_____

_____

Today I am truly grateful for...

_____

_____

_____

_____

Here's what would make today great...

_____

_____

_____

_____

I am...

_____

_____

Some amazing things that happened today...

_____

_____

Some amazing things that happened today... ✨ ✨ 🌙

_____

_____

What could I have done to make today even better?

_____

_____

Date: _____

☀

Quote Of The Day

_____
_____
_____

Today I am truly grateful for...

_____
_____
_____
_____
_____

Here's what would make today great...

_____
_____
_____
_____
_____

I am...

_____
_____
_____

Some amazing things that happened today...

_____
_____

Some amazing things that happened today...

_____
_____
_____

What could I have done to make today even better?

_____
_____

Date:

Quote Of The Day

_____

_____

Today I am truly grateful for...

_____

_____

_____

_____

Here's what would make today great...

_____

_____

_____

_____

I am...

_____

_____

Some amazing things that happened today...

_____

_____

Some amazing things that happened today...

_____

_____

What could I have done to make today even better?

_____

_____

Date: ....

Quote Of The Day

_____

_____

_____

Today I am truly grateful for...

_____

_____

_____

_____

_____

Here's what would make today great...

_____

_____

_____

_____

_____

I am...

_____

_____

Some amazing things that happened today...

_____

_____

Some amazing things that happened today...

_____

_____

What could I have done to make today even better?

_____

Date:

Quote Of The Day

_____

_____

_____

Today I am truly grateful for...

_____

_____

_____

_____

Here's what would make today great...

_____

_____

_____

_____

I am...

_____

_____

Some amazing things that happened today...

_____

Some amazing things that happened today...

_____

_____

What could I have done to make today even better?

_____

Date: _____

☀

Quote Of The Day

_____
_____
_____

Today I am truly grateful for...

_____
_____
_____
_____
_____

Here's what would make today great...

_____
_____
_____
_____
_____

I am...

_____
_____
_____

Some amazing things that happened today...

_____
_____

Some amazing things that happened today...   ✨ ✨ 🌙

_____
_____

What could I have done to make today even better?

_____
_____

Date:

☀

Quote Of The Day

_____

_____

_____

Today I am truly grateful for...

_____

_____

_____

_____

_____

_____

Here's what would make today great...

_____

_____

_____

_____

_____

_____

I am...

_____

_____

_____

Some amazing things that happened today...

_____

_____

Some amazing things that happened today...

_____

_____

What could I have done to make today even better?

_____

_____

Date: _____

Quote Of The Day

_____

_____

Today I am truly grateful for...

_____

_____

_____

_____

_____

Here's what would make today great...

_____

_____

_____

_____

_____

I am...

_____

_____

_____

Some amazing things that happened today...

_____

_____

Some amazing things that happened today...

_____

_____

_____

What could I have done to make today even better?

_____

_____

Date: _____

Quote Of The Day

_____
_____

Today I am truly grateful for...

_____
_____
_____
_____

Here's what would make today great...

_____
_____
_____
_____

I am...

_____
_____

Some amazing things that happened today...

_____
_____

Some amazing things that happened today...

_____
_____

What could I have done to make today even better?

_____

Date:

Quote Of The Day

_____

_____

_____

Today I am truly grateful for...

_____

_____

_____

_____

_____

Here's what would make today great...

_____

_____

_____

_____

_____

I am...

_____

_____

_____

Some amazing things that happened today...

_____

_____

Some amazing things that happened today...

_____

_____

What could I have done to make today even better?

_____

_____

Date:

Quote Of The Day

_____
_____

_____

Today I am truly grateful for...

_____
_____

_____
_____

_____

Here's what would make today great...

_____
_____

_____
_____

_____

I am...

_____
_____

_____

Some amazing things that happened today...

_____
_____

Some amazing things that happened today...

_____
_____

What could I have done to make today even better?

_____
_____

Date: _____

Quote Of The Day

_____
_____
_____

Today I am truly grateful for...

_____
_____
_____
_____
_____

Here's what would make today great...

_____
_____
_____
_____
_____

I am...

_____
_____
_____

Some amazing things that happened today...

_____
_____

Some amazing things that happened today...

_____
_____

What could I have done to make today even better?

_____
_____

Date:

Quote Of The Day

_____

_____

Today I am truly grateful for...

_____

_____

_____

_____

Here's what would make today great...

_____

_____

_____

_____

I am...

_____

_____

Some amazing things that happened today...

_____

_____

Some amazing things that happened today...

_____

_____

What could I have done to make today even better?

_____

Date: _____

Quote Of The Day

_____
_____

Today I am truly grateful for...

_____
_____
_____
_____
_____

Here's what would make today great...

_____
_____
_____
_____
_____

I am...

_____
_____
_____

Some amazing things that happened today...

_____
_____

Some amazing things that happened today...

_____
_____

What could I have done to make today even better?

_____
_____

Date: _____

Quote Of The Day

_____
_____

Today I am truly grateful for...

_____
_____
_____
_____
_____

Here's what would make today great...

_____
_____
_____
_____
_____

I am...

_____
_____
_____

Some amazing things that happened today...

_____
_____

Some amazing things that happened today...

_____
_____
_____

What could I have done to make today even better?

_____
_____

Date:

Quote Of The Day

_____

_____

Today I am truly grateful for...

_____

_____

_____

_____

Here's what would make today great...

_____

_____

_____

_____

I am...

_____

_____

Some amazing things that happened today...

_____

_____

Some amazing things that happened today...

_____

_____

_____

What could I have done to make today even better?

_____

_____

Date:

Quote Of The Day

_____

_____

Today I am truly grateful for...

_____

_____

_____

_____

Here's what would make today great...

_____

_____

_____

_____

I am...

_____

_____

Some amazing things that happened today...

_____

_____

Some amazing things that happened today...

_____

_____

What could I have done to make today even better?

_____

_____

Date: _____   ☀

Quote Of The Day
_____
_____
_____

Today I am truly grateful for...
_____
_____
_____
_____
_____

Here's what would make today great...
_____
_____
_____
_____
_____

I am...
_____
_____
_____

Some amazing things that happened today...
_____
_____

Some amazing things that happened today...   ✨ ✨ 🌙
_____
_____

What could I have done to make today even better?
_____
_____

Date: _____ ☀

Quote Of The Day

_____
_____
_____

Today I am truly grateful for...

_____
_____
_____
_____
_____

Here's what would make today great...

_____
_____
_____
_____
_____

I am...

_____
_____
_____

Some amazing things that happened today...

_____
_____

Some amazing things that happened today...

_____
_____
_____

What could I have done to make today even better?

_____
_____

Date: ─────────────────

Quote Of The Day

───

───

Today I am truly grateful for...

───

───

───

───

Here's what would make today great...

───

───

───

───

I am...

───

───

───

Some amazing things that happened today...

───

───

Some amazing things that happened today...

───

───

What could I have done to make today even better?

───

Date:

Quote Of The Day

_____

_____

Today I am truly grateful for...

_____

_____

_____

_____

Here's what would make today great...

_____

_____

_____

_____

I am...

_____

_____

Some amazing things that happened today...

_____

_____

Some amazing things that happened today...

_____

_____

What could I have done to make today even better?

_____

_____

Date: ....

Quote Of The Day

_____

_____

_____

Today I am truly grateful for...

_____

_____

_____

_____

_____

Here's what would make today great...

_____

_____

_____

_____

_____

I am...

_____

_____

_____

Some amazing things that happened today...

_____

_____

Some amazing things that happened today...

_____

_____

What could I have done to make today even better?

_____

_____

Date:

Quote Of The Day

_____
_____
_____

Today I am truly grateful for...

_____
_____
_____
_____
_____

Here's what would make today great...

_____
_____
_____
_____
_____

I am...

_____
_____
_____

Some amazing things that happened today...

_____
_____

Some amazing things that happened today...

_____
_____

What could I have done to make today even better?

_____
_____

Date:

Quote Of The Day

_____

_____

_____

Today I am truly grateful for...

_____

_____

_____

_____

_____

Here's what would make today great...

_____

_____

_____

_____

_____

I am...

_____

_____

_____

Some amazing things that happened today...

_____

_____

Some amazing things that happened today...

_____

_____

What could I have done to make today even better?

_____

_____

Date: _____

Quote Of The Day

_____
_____
_____

Today I am truly grateful for...

_____
_____
_____
_____
_____

Here's what would make today great...

_____
_____
_____
_____
_____

I am...

_____
_____
_____

Some amazing things that happened today...

_____
_____

Some amazing things that happened today...

_____
_____

What could I have done to make today even better?

_____
_____

Made in the USA
Las Vegas, NV
07 May 2023